FREAKY PHENOMENA

MYSTERIOUS PLACES

The Series

CONSCIOUSNESS
FAITH
HEALING
LIFE AFTER DEATH
MYSTERIOUS PLACES
PERSONALITY
PSYCHIC ABILITIES
THE SENSES

FREAKY PHENOMENA

MYSTERIOUS PLACES

Don Rauf

Foreword by Joe Nickell, Senior Research Fellow, Committee for Skeptical Inquiry

MASON CREST

Mason Crest
450 Parkway Drive, Suite D Broomall, PA 19008
www.masoncrest.com

Printed in the United States of America

First printing
9 8 7 6 5 4 3 2 1

Series ISBN: 978-1-4222-3772-4
Hardcover ISBN: 978-1-4222-3777-9
ebook ISBN: 978-1-4222-8011-9

Cataloging-in-Publication Data is available on file at the Library of Congress.

Developed and Produced by Print Matters Productions, Inc. (www.printmattersinc.com)
Cover and Interior Design by: Bill Madrid, Madrid Design
Composition by Carling Design

Picture credits: 9, scnhnc052008/Shutterstock; 10, WitR/Shutterstock; 12, Orhan Cam/Shutterstock; 14, nihatdursun/iStock; 15, Aloya3/iStock; 17, tr3gin/Shutterstock; 18, Roman Babakin/Shutterstock; 21, SheraleeS/iStock; 21, Morphart Creation/Shutterstock; 22, NeonLight/Shutterstock; 23, SIYAMA9/iStock; 24, david ruiz martin/Shutterstock; 25, Abner Veltier/Shutterstock; 28, Gfed/iStock; 29, Christhilf/iStock; 30, Grant M Henderson/Shutterstock; 32, Kisialiou Yury/Shutterstock; 35, By Photograph was taken by the New York Navy Yard via Wikimedia Commons; 36, National Tansportation Safety Board; 36, National Tansportation Safety Board; 38, By NASA via Wikimedia Commons; 39, sipaphoto/iStock; 41, CIA.gov; 42, Stock image/Shutterstock; 43, Wikimedia Commons; 43, CrackerClips Stock Media/Shutterstock

Cover: merydolla/Shutterstock

CONTENTS

KEY ICONS TO LOOK FOR:

Words to understand: These words with their easy-to-understand definitions will increase the reader's understanding of the text while building vocabulary skills.

Sidebars: This boxed material within the main text allows readers to build knowledge, gain insights, explore possibilities, and broaden their perspectives by weaving together additional information to provide realistic and holistic perspectives.

Educational Videos: Readers can view videos by scanning our QR codes, providing them with additional educational content to supplement the text. Examples include news coverage, moments in history, speeches, iconic sports moments and much more!

Series glossary of key terms: This back-of-the book glossary contains terminology used throughout this series. Words found here increase the reader's ability to read and comprehend higher-level books and articles in this field.

Advice From a Full-Time Professional Investigator of Strange Mysteries

I wish I'd had books like this when I was young. Like other boys and girls, I was intrigued by ghosts, monsters, and other freaky things. I grew up to become a stage magician and private detective, as well as (among other things) a literary and folklore scholar and a forensic-science writer. By 1995, I was using my varied background as the world's only full-time professional investigator of strange mysteries.

As I travel around the world, lured by its enigmas, I avoid both uncritical belief and outright dismissal. I insist mysteries should be *investigated* with the intent of solving them. That requires *critical thinking*, which begins by asking useful questions. I share three such questions here, applied to brief cases from my own files:

Is a particular story really true?

Consider Louisiana's Myrtles Plantation, supposedly haunted by the ghost of a murderous slave, Chloe. We are told that, as revenge against a cruel master, she poisoned three members of his family. Phenomena that ghost hunters attributed to her spirit included a mysteriously swinging door and unexplained banging noises.

The Discovery TV Channel arranged for me to spend a night there alone. I learned from the local historical society that Chloe never existed and her three alleged victims actually died in a yellow fever epidemic. I prowled the house, discovering that the spooky door was simply hung off center, and that banging noises were easily explained by a loose shutter.

Does a claim involve unnecessary assumptions?

In Flatwoods, WV, in 1952, some boys saw a fiery UFO streak across the evening sky and apparently land on a hill. They went looking for it, joined by others. A flashlight soon revealed a tall creature with shining eyes and a face shaped like the ace of spades. Suddenly, it swooped at them with "terrible claws," making a high-pitched hissing sound. The witnesses fled for their lives.

Half a century later, I talked with elderly residents, examined old newspaper accounts, and did other research. I learned the UFO had been a meteor. Descriptions of the creature almost perfectly matched a barn owl—seemingly tall because it had perched on a tree limb. In contrast, numerous incredible assumptions would be required to argue for a flying saucer and an alien being.

Is the proof as great as the claim?

A Canadian woman sometimes exhibited the crucifixion wounds of Jesus—allegedly produced supernaturally. In 2002, I watched blood stream from her hands and feet and from tiny scalp wounds like those from a crown of thorns.

However, because her wounds were already bleeding, they could have been self-inflicted. The lance wound that pierced Jesus' side was absent, and the supposed nail wounds did not pass through the hands and feet, being only on one side of each. Getting a closer look, I saw that one hand wound was only a small slit, not a large puncture wound. Therefore, this extraordinary claim lacked the extraordinary proof required.

These three questions should prove helpful in approaching claims and tales in Freaky Phenomena. I view the progress of science as a continuing series of solved mysteries. Perhaps you too might consider a career as a science detective. You can get started right here.

Joe Nickell
Senior Research Fellow, Committee for Skeptical Inquiry
Amherst, NY

STRANGE FORCES AT WORK

The world is a mysterious place, and certain spots on our planet are certainly more mysterious than others. At a few locations around the globe, for example, gravity seems to have gone crazy. At locales called "gravity hills," drivers can put their car into neutral at the base of an incline, and then their vehicle seems to magically roll up the slope. While gravity hills may appear to defy the laws of physics, they are likely an optical illusion of the landscape—objects only appear to be going uphill.

But the scientific explanation doesn't sway believers in the supernatural, who attribute the forces at gravity hills to otherworldly spirits. Legends hold that cars in these mystery zones go uphill in neutral because they are moved by the force of ghosts. The typical story is that long ago a school bus broke down on the site. The children got out of the bus to push it up the hill, but it rolled backward and crushed them to death. Their ghosts are now reliving the moment for eternity—pushing cars up the hill.

There are mystery spots dotting the globe, such as The Mystery Spot in Santa Cruz, CA. In this circular area in the redwood forest, billiard balls travel up slopes, water pours up to the sky, chairs appear to rest on walls, compasses act strangely, and people seem to be able to stand at impossible angles. One creative explanation is that a UFO buried deep in the ground has been causing the inexplicable occurrences. But there are a couple of more likely reasons, such as geo-physical anomalies—natural forces, such as magnetism or gravity, that are unusually strong in a particular spot. Or again, may be simply an optical illusion.

Although these gravity zones are certainly intriguing, other places may hold even greater secrets and pose bigger questions. Take the pyramids of Egypt. How were they erected thou-

sands of years ago from stones often weighing several tons? Or Stonehenge in England. Were the huge monoliths erected to serve a unique purpose connected to the sun and moon? Who built the giant mysterious heads on Easter Island in Polynesia? Why have so many planes and ships vanished in an area of the Atlantic Ocean called the Bermuda Triangle? Does a military base in the Nevada desert house alien technology and proof of life from beyond our planet? Join us as we explore some of these mysterious places around the world.

The Christ of the Abyss is a submerged, bronze statue of Jesus Christ located in the San Fruttuoso Bay in Italy. Although it is known who the sculptor was and why it was placed in this particular spot, it is still an unusual sight for divers.

CHAPTER 1

PYRAMIDS

The pyramids in Egypt are among the most remarkable structures in the world. These massive structures continue to be studied by scholars and are frequently visited by tourists.

Near the Nile River on the Giza Plateau not far from Egypt's capital city of Cairo stand the pyramids, long considered among the greatest wonders of the world. More than 100 pyramids remain in Egypt. They all have four triangular sides rising from a square base and meeting at a point. The Giza pyramids were built between 2589 BCE and 2504 BCE, a period of 85 years, during a time known as the Pyramid Age. Guarded by the Great Sphinx of Giza (a sphinx is a mythical creature with the body of a lion and the head of a human), the Great Pyramid of Cheops, also called Khufu, is perhaps the most famous, and the largest pyramid ever built. It is the only surviving "wonder" of the Seven Wonders of the Ancient World (as defined by the engineer and writer Philo of Byzantium in 225 BCE). The Great Pyramid was the focal point of a complex that featured several small pyramids, boat pits, a mortuary temple, and flat-roofed tombs.

Why Were They Built?

The predominant archaeological theory, which Herodotus, a fifth-century Greek from the democratic city of Athens, put forth is that the pyramids are immense tombs for kings from this period. Those on the Giza Plateau were built for the **pharaohs** Khufu, Khafre, and Menkaure. Ancient Egyptians viewed

Words to Understand

Mummify: To shrivel and dry up and thus preserve a dead body or thing.

Papyrus: A material prepared in ancient Egypt from the pithy stem of a water plant, used to make sheets for writing or painting on, rope, sandals, and boats.

Parapsychologist: A person who studies paranormal and psychic phenomena.

Pharaoh: A ruler in ancient Egypt.

Reconstitute: To restore or reconstruct by adding water.

Sarcophagus: A stone coffin especially associated with the ancient civilizations of Egypt, Rome, and Greece.

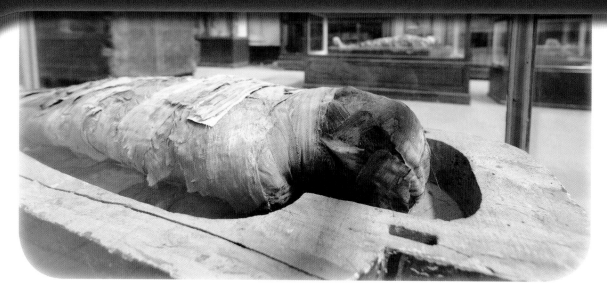

Archaeologists have discovered the remains of ancient Egyptian pharaohs in burial chambers under pyramids. Some of these sarcophaguses have been excavated and can be found in glass display cases in museums around the world.

their pharaohs as living gods. These pyramids represented a link between heaven and earth. They were the launching pads for souls to reach heaven.

The ancient Egyptians believed in the afterlife. The treatment of the dead in this world was essential to eternal life after death. They believed that when they died they would stand before the god Osiris and 42 judges. On Judgment Day, their heart supposedly would be placed on one side of a scale and a feather would be placed on the other side, and the gods would gauge whether a person's heart was heavy with sin.

Each pyramid contained a series of burial chambers, ventilation shafts, and passageways. The pharaoh's **sarcophagus** was placed in the king's burial chamber, along with items that might be needed in the afterlife: gold, favorite objects, and pottery.

Throughout history, scholars have debated how exactly the pyramids were built. Take the Great Pyramid, for example. When it was erected, it stood about 480 feet tall or about the size of a 44-story building. Until 1887 when the Eiffel Tower was completed, it was the tallest structure on the planet. It has a base measuring 592,000 square feet or about 13.5 acres.

Each of the pyramid's four walls measured together as a straight line add up to 36,524 inches. Interestingly, the exact length of a year is 365.24 days. The four sides of the pyramid are slightly concave. Remarkably, the bow created by these stone blocks matches the exact curvature of the Earth.

If the circumference of the pyramid is divided by twice its height (the diameter of a circle is twice the radius), the result is 3.14159, which happens to be the mathematical constant known as pi.

About 2,300,000 stone blocks ranging in weight from 2 to 70 tons each were used to construct the pyramid. Originally, it was covered entirely in white limestone, and its very smooth surface and seams that were almost undetectable made it impossible to climb. The flat and highly polished surface reflected the sun's rays and made the pyramid shine like a jewel or giant mirrors in the desert. In fact, the ancient Egyptians called the Great Pyramid *Ikhet* or Glorious Light.

The structure is oriented almost perfectly to the north. Glen Dash, an engineer who studies the pyramids at Giza as part of Ancient Egypt Research Associates (AERA), has noted that Khufu's pyramid is aligned to true north within one-tenth of a degree. The structure also stands at the exact center of the Earth's land mass at a point of 30 degrees longitude and 30 degrees latitude. It is also positioned so that on the first day of the spring equinox, March 21, the north face disappears in shadow at exactly noon. American author Peter Tompkins saw the pyramid as a huge clock. Others have thought it was a type of observatory.

Learn more about the secrets of the pyramids.

How Were They Constructed?

The ancient Egyptian civilization was quite advanced. They were skilled boatbuilders and astronomers. They developed the concept of the 12-month calendar year and a way of writing, produced art and architecture, and made advances in farming. But even though these ancient people had a great deal of knowledge, scholars have puzzled over how they built the enormous structures.

Historians used to believe that the pharoah Khufu (also known as Cheops) used an army of slaves to haul and place the stones. Today, scientists and historians believe that 20,000 to 30,000 volunteers and paid laborers moved the massive stones from quarries located hundreds of miles away. A June 2016 article in Live Science explains that ancient records kept on **papyrus** show that many of the limestone blocks were shipped by boat along canals and the Nile River to ports in Giza.

It is suspected that the laborers were well fed. A report published by AERA estimates that enough cattle and goats were slaughtered every day to produce 4,000 pounds of meat to feed the pyramid workers. Also, the laborers worked in teams. Group names have been found—carved in the stones at the Great Pyramid—such as The Pure Ones of Khufu, Those Who Know Unas (the name of another pyramid complex), and The Drunks of Menkaure.

Workers in Egypt may have transported stone blocks using ropes.

The ancient Egyptians recorded histories and myths on papyrus scrolls.

Even with masses of workers on the job, how did they move such heavy stones great distances? In 2014, researchers at the University of Amsterdam wrote: "For the construction of the pyramids, the ancient Egyptians had to transport heavy blocks of stone and large statues across the desert. The Egyptians therefore placed the heavy objects on a sledge that workers pulled over the sand. Research . . . revealed that the Egyptians probably made the desert sand in front of the sledge wet."

The sledges were basically large wooden sleds, on which were placed tons of heavy stones, dragged through the desert by human laborers and oxen. The scientists said that wetting the sand cut the pulling force required in half. Other Egyptology experts have explained that the massive stones were hauled along tracks of round logs placed beneath the sledges. The logs acted as rollers to move the rocks along.

While there were no cranes, pulleys, and steel cables as there are today, workers employed levers, papyrus ropes, and sheer sweat and muscle to put the rocks into position. The super human achievement took a physical toll. When archaeologists excavated 600 tombs of people believed to have worked on the tombs, they noted that the skeletons were severely stressed and damaged, indicating wear and tear from heavy labor.

Scientific Take:
Exact Stone Cutting and Possible Molding

The pyramid stones themselves were cut and fitted with great precision. The right angles are at a perfect 90 degrees. The gaps between the stones are so tight that a knife cannot even fit between them. The gaps were filled with a mortar that has survived the test of time—lasting through heat, cold, storms, earthquakes, and more. Although it has been analyzed, scientists can still not figure out its composition.

Egyptologists have presumed that the stones themselves were cut with bronze chisels and other tools. Yet none of these tools have ever been found in the Giza Plateau. Another theory about the stones is that some may have not been from a quarry at all but were cast with a form of concrete. Dr. Michel Barsoum, a professor in the Department of Materials Science and Engineering at Drexel University in Philadelphia, conducted analysis on several pyramid stones and concluded that their composition was consistent with **reconstituted** limestone. He speculates that workers took pulverized limestone and mixed it with water, lime, clay, and salt in molds to create the perfect building blocks. Barsoum and his colleagues say that casting the stones would explain why they fit so perfectly together. The theory has been supported by several other scientists.

Pyramid Power

One notion that has intrigued writers and investigators is that the very structure of the pyramid holds mysterious power. In the 1930s, the Frenchman Andre Bovis found that animals that happened to get trapped in the pyramids and die did not decompose. Wanting to see if the

The Nazca Lines

In Peru, about 200 miles south of Lima, more than 10,000 lines were etched into the desert sands over 2,000 years ago. When viewed at ground level, the lines don't look very remarkable, but from nearby hilltops or the air, these lines come together to form 300 geometric figures and 70 images of plants and animals, including a monkey, a condor, a lizard, a spider, and a dog. Author Erich von Däniken and other investigators believe that the lines are the handiwork of beings from outer space. How else can you explain that they are only visible from high in the air? One scientific explanation is that they can be seen from nearby foothills, and so they serve as directional markers for ceremonial sites.

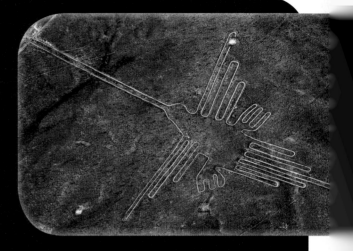

This photo shows an aerial view of the Nazca Line Hummingbird.

pyramid structure held special power, he created a small model, aligned it due north, and put a dead cat inside. After several days, Bovis discovered that the animal corpse shrank, dried, and became **mummified**.

In 1949, Karel Drbal of Czechoslovakia filed a patent on a small pyramid that was to be used to sharpen razor blades. Drbal claimed that placing dull blades in a pyramid-shaped container for several days returned them to a sharpened state. The TV show *MythBusters* tried the experiment and found that blades do not seem to get any sharper in the pyramid.

In the 1970s, Max Toth, hypnotist and **parapsychologist**, claimed that seeds germinated faster when placed beneath a model pyramid. American author and inventor G. Pat Flanagan claimed that pyramids affected food, taking the bite from bitter items, making coffee taste smoother, and intensifying sweetness. During a burst of interest in New Age Spiritualism, tubular pyramid structures were sold, under which users could meditate.

CHAPTER 2

STONEHENGE

Stonehenge is one of the wonders of the world and a well-known prehistoric monument.

n the English countryside at Wiltshire, just about two hours west of London, a collection of 93 small and very large stones form a circular pattern that has puzzled humans for thousands of years. The mysterious **monoliths** attract about 850,000 visitors every year. The monument makes an impressive sight. Monolithic **sarsen** sandstones rise 30 feet tall and weigh about 25 tons. Today, 17 of these mammoth rocks stand upright. Many of the sarsen stones were placed in a formation that is now an iconic image of Stonehenge: two upright sarsen stones with one placed across the top (called the **lintel**) to form a **trilithon** (coming from the Greek for "three stones"). Just three of the trilithon lintels still rest upon their upright stones. Surrounding the trilithons were 30 **megalith** stones that formed a partial circle, with 30 lintels on top.

Scientific Take: How Did the Stones Get There?

When visiting Stonehenge today, you will also see shorter stones called *bluestones*, which have a bluish hue when wet or broken. Currently, 43 remain at the site, although they numbered 60 when they were originally placed there. While scientists believe that the large sarsen stones were found locally (similar sandstone can be found just 18 miles north), the bluestones are more of a puzzle. Scientists have determined that they are made of spotted dolerite, only found about 150 miles away in the Preseli Mountains of Wales. Although the bluestones originated at such a great distance from the site,

Words to Understand

Lintel: A horizontal support of timber, stone, concrete, or steel across the top of a door, window, or other structure.

Megalith: A large stone that forms a prehistoric monument.

Monolith: A giant, single upright block of stone, especially as a monument.

Sarsen: A type of sandstone boulder found in the chalk downs of southern England.

Trilithon: A structure made from two large vertical stones (posts) supporting a third stone set horizontally across the top (lintel).

geologists have thought that workers somehow transported them from the mountains.

Watch a National Geographic documentary on Stonehenge.

Another theory, however, suggests that glaciers could have moved the rocks. In 1971, the English geologist Geoffrey Kellaway published a study in *Nature* indicating that these special rocks could have been moved to the Salisbury Plain by glaciers. An article published in *Earth Magazine* in 2008 said that the convergence of the two glaciers "acted as a conveyor belt, transporting erratics in a trail leading straight to Stonehenge." *Erratics* are rocks or boulders that differ from the surrounding rock, believed to have been brought from a distance by glacial action.

Moving Mammoth Stones

Even though the sarsens were located relatively close to the Stonehenge site, they weighed many tons. Just as with the stones comprising Egyptians pyramids, scholars have wondered how early man could haul such heavy stones with primitive means. Scientists think the builders of Stonehenge may have used sleds or pushed them along on rollers made of large tree trunks—in a manner similar to the Egyptians.

Archaeologists have found tools made of stone that were used to carve the megaliths into their shapes. The Stonehenge creators used these "hammerstones" to pound the larger rocks and chip off pieces. Researchers have marveled at the precision that went into many of these big stones. For example, the lintel stones that topped the outer ring of sarsen stones fit together tightly using *tongue-and-groove joints*, and they were perfectly horizontal even though the ground was uneven. The tops on the sarsen stones had protrusions and the lintels had holes. Like a primitive form of Lego block, the protrusion and the hole helped secure the stones tightly together. Using a system of large wooden poles, timber platforms, and ropes, the workers of old were able to raise and position the stones.

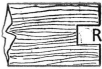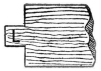

Researchers believe that log rollers (left) were used to move the massive stones that make up Stonehenge. Tongue-and-groove joints (below) are often used in woodworking.

The Who and the Why

The monoliths known as Stonehenge date back 4,000 to 5,000 years to the late Stone Age or early Bronze Age, an era long before the Vikings or the Romans arrived in Britain. Historians have speculated that the entire structure was built in stages from 3000 BCE to 1500 BCE.

Prehistoric Britons built the structure for reasons unknown to us, although there have been many theories. Historians have thought the region was considered sacred land well before Stonehenge was constructed. In a 2014 issue of *Live Science*, an article reported that three large pine posts, which were totem poles of sorts, were erected at the site as early as 10,500 years ago, indicating that this area had spiritual significance. Stone circles are common throughout the British Isles and Brittany. Researchers have documented about 1,300 such sites, although they estimate around 4,000 were originally created. Stonehenge has gained the most attention for its size and artful construction.

There have been several theories about the purpose of the structure. In the *Live Science* article, University of Birmingham archaeologist Vincent Gaffney states that Stonehenge was part of a complex landscape connected to processional and ritual activities. An archaeological study from the University College London published in the journal *Antiquity* in 2016 suggests that Stonehenge was used as a burial ground and a cremation cemetery based on charred skeletons that were found there. Archeologists estimate that the remains of 240 people may be buried at Stonehenge.

The Sarsen Circle is in the form of a horseshoe with the open side facing northeast.

Those buried at the site were likely prominent members of their society, according to the archeologist Mike Parker Pearson, former director of the Riverside Stonehenge Project. Archaeologists have long speculated about whether Stonehenge was put up by prehistoric chiefs—perhaps even ancient royalty—and the new results suggest that not only is this likely to have been the case but it also was the resting place of their mortal remains.

Healing, Protection, Fertility: Possible Purposes of Stonehenge

Because several of the skeletons found at the site show signs of illness or injury, some scientists have thought that ancient people came to the location for its healing properties. Other researchers have proposed that it was a fortress for the protection of local citizens, while another group has theorized it might have been a fertility temple.

A Connection to the Heavens

In 1965, scientist Gerald Hawkins, a professor of astronomy at Boston University, discovered about 165 connections between Stonehenge and events in the sky. Because of alignments with the sun and moon, Stonehenge might be considered an ancient astronomical observatory.

Hawkins believed the structure could be used as a calendar and to predict important solar and lunar events. A sightline that runs through one trilithon aligns with the winter solstice sunset. The horseshoe of stones also opens up in the direction of the summer solstice sunrise.

If you sit at the center on the day of the solstice, you have a clear view of the sun rising over a large sarsen stone called the Heel Stone, which stands outside the primary collection of stones. The rays of the sun shine into the center of the monument. Other trilithon doorways and stones line up with the moon at different times of the year. The Aubrey Holes are a series of chalk pits that circle the inner bank of Stonehenge. Hawkins proposed that the holes could be used to predict lunar eclipses. Others have thought that these holes were related to fertility cycles.

Stonehenge could have been an astronomical observatory.

CHAPTER 3

EASTER ISLAND

Easter Island is one of the most remote
inhabited islands in the world.

solated in the Pacific Ocean about 2,300 miles off the west coast of Chile, Easter Island is so remote that it's hard to believe anyone settled there. Just 64 square miles in size (or about three times the size of Manhattan), Easter Island is 4,300 miles southeast of Hawaii and about 2,500 miles from Tahiti. Its nearest neighbor is the tiny Pitcairn Island, where the **mutineers** from the *HMS Bounty* and their Polynesian friends and families settled in 1790, is more than 1,200 miles away.

The first inhabitants of Rapa Nui (the native name of the island) are believed to have come to the island in 400 CE, led by their great chief, Hotu Matu'a. Most likely they originated from other Polynesian islands—more than 1,000 make up the region in the southern and central Pacific Ocean.

There are some 900 giant carved figures on the island.

Words to Understand

Anthropologist: A professional who studies the origin, development, and behavioral aspects of human beings and their societies, especially primitive societies.

Archaeologist: A person who studies human history and prehistory through the excavation of sites and the analysis of artifacts and other physical remains found.

Mutineer: A person, especially a soldier or sailor, who rebels or refuses to obey the orders of a person in authority.

Pumice: A very light and porous volcanic rock used to smooth or clean.

Despite the island's isolated locale, an estimated 80,000 tourists visit each year. The attraction: about 900 giant carved stone figures that gaze out from various locations. The Rapa Nui natives, who built the giant stone heads, left no written history, so the purpose and meaning of the large silent heads have remained a mystery.

Land of the Giant Heads

When Dutch explorers, led by admiral Jacob Roggeveen, arrived there in 1722, they named the land for the day they arrived: Easter Sunday. Imagine their reaction when they saw the hundreds of massive megaliths that the Rapa Nui call moai.

Scientists have determined that the ancient Polynesians carved the moai between 1100 and 1500 CE. While the moai range in size from just a few feet tall to 72 feet (named El Gigante), an average monolith stands 13 feet tall and weighs about 14 tons. El Gigante weighs more than two jet airliners, although it lies unfinished. Paro is the largest standing moai at 33 feet and weighing 75 metric tons.

Standing with their faces away from the ocean, the giant heads represent the spirits of ancestors, chiefs, or other high-ranking males who held important positions, according to *Nova*, the PBS documentary series. **Archaeologist** and Easter Island expert Jo Anne Van Tilburg

Surprise! Bodies below the Heads

Because the most famous pictures of the moai appear to be of only a head and shoulders, people had thought that those images showed whole Easter Island statues. But archaeologists have dug beneath the ground to reveal that these statues indeed have torsos beneath their heads, most with arms hanging down to the side and their thin fingers stretching across their stomachs. In addition, there are moai on the island that already stand above ground on flat mounds or stone pedestals called *ahus*, a word that also means "sacred ceremonial site."

believes that the heads are representations of island chiefs, and that tribespeople most likely carved a new head each time an important tribal figure died. The moai all look similar with their heavy brows, long earlobes, big noses, and thin pouting lips. Several of the statues also sport what appear to be red hats, although historians say they may represent hair.

Find out more about Easter Island in the documentary, *The Secret Unsolved Mystery of Easter Island.*

Forged from Volcanic Rock

No two Easter Island figures look exactly alike. The huge statues were carved from the island's volcanic rock with simple handheld chisels called *toki* and then rubbed smooth with **pumice**.

Almost all the monoliths are thought to come from the volcanic quarry called Rano Raraku. Archaeologists say the ancient islanders turned the volcanic crater into a moai factory, and visitors today can see hundreds of moai that are still lying facing skyward at the top of Rano Raraku, where they were carved but never erected.

Scientific Take: Moving Mountains

As with the stones of the pyramids and Stonehenge, people have wondered how the primitive tribespeople carried out the Herculean task of moving and erecting the mammoth monoliths. A number of the carved stones appear to have been transported up to 11 miles from the quarry. Scientists have theorized that, just as with the Egyptians and early people of Stonehenge, the natives used log rollers, ropes, and wooden sledges.

Recently, a pair of archaeologists came up with a new theory: Perhaps the statues were engineered to move upright in a rocking motion, using only manpower and rope. In 2012, researchers from the University of Hawaii and California State University, Long Beach proved the feasibility of the idea. As reported in *National Geographic*, the scientists demonstrated how the

Rano Kau is an extinct volcano crater on Easter Island. The crater contains several igneous rocks including obsidian and pumice, used by the island's stoneworkers.

large statues could be maneuvered by a team of 18 people, rolling and rocking the monoliths and moving them along with a bit of rope.

In 1986, the Norwegian explorer-adventurer Thor Heyerdahl and Czech engineer Pavel Pavel demonstrated how the statues could be set upright and walked forward with the muscle of 17 workers using a twisting motion. While no one is quite sure, the accomplishment of moving the monoliths was a monumental task. In *National Geographic*, a Rapa Nui native explained how it was really done: "We know the truth," said the tour guide. "The statues walked."

Why Did the Island People Die Out?

Scientists have determined that when the first native Polynesian people arrived at Easter Island it was covered with trees, even though there is very little freshwater and the soil is poor, lacking in minerals. There may have been as many as 16 million trees, including several species that reached 100 feet high. When Dutch explorers first arrived in the eighteenth century, the human population was estimated to be about 3,000. At its height, 20,000 people may have lived on Easter Island.

One theory about why the population suddenly declined holds that around 1200 CE inhabitants began cutting down giant palms and other trees to build boats and to farm, and the practice eventually cleared the island of almost all its trees. Two **anthropologists**, Terry Hunt and Carl Lipo, from the University of Hawaii, have a different theory, however. They suggest that Polynesian rats are to blame for decimating the trees. They had stowed away on the canoes of the original settlers. Once on the island, they multiplied at a furious rate (rat populations can double within two months), and then binge-ate the roots of the palms. Hunt has presented evidence that the island's rat population spiked to 20 million between the years 1200 and 1300.

With contact from the West, the native population declined even faster. The European visitors brought smallpox and syphilis, which wiped out a large portion of the Rapa Nui natives. In addition to those lost to disease, an estimated 1,000 to 1,400 islanders were captured and taken away by Peruvian and Spanish slave raiders in the 1800s. The population was down to 111 by 1877. Today, it is roughly 3,300—about the same as when the European explorers first arrived.

Although the population on Easter Island has swiftly declined, there are still some native people who live there and continue the traditions of their Polynesian ancestors.

CHAPTER 4

THE BERMUDA TRIANGLE

The Bermuda Triangle is said to be responsible for many mysterious plane and shipwrecks.

In the past 100 years, at least 20 planes and 50 ships have gone missing in a triangular area stretching from Puerto Rico to Bermuda to Florida called the Bermuda Triangle (also referred to as the Devil's Triangle). While plane crashes and shipwrecks do occur at sea, the peculiar aspect in this area is that craft often have vanished without a trace. Travelers have noted strange happenings in the Triangle for centuries. In the 1400s, the explorer Christopher Columbus wrote about inexplicable occurrences in this region—his ships' compasses not working normally and spotting what appeared to be a strange ball of fire in an area near the Bermuda Triangle.

Theories behind the Bermuda Triangle phenomena are many. The language expert Charles Berlitz, who wrote a best-selling book about the Triangle in 1974, believed that the legendary and mythic island of Atlantis plays a role in the disturbances within the Triangle. Others think that there is a rift in space and time in the Bermuda Triangle and the lost planes and ships have slipped into another dimension. American pilot Bruce Gernon believes that a type of time portal exists in the region. During a routine trip from the Bahamas to Florida on December 4, 1970, a strange cloud surrounded Gernon's plane and his compass began spinning out of control. He later wrote:

Words to Understand

Debris: Scattered pieces of waste or remains.

Peninsula: A piece of land almost surrounded by water or projecting out into a body of water except for a section connecting it with the mainland.

Squadron: An operational unit in an air force consisting of two or more flights of aircraft.

Squall: A sudden violent gust of wind or a localized storm.

Transmission: The act or process of sending electrical signals to a radio, television, computer, or other device.

We were in the tunnel [of magnetic fog] for only 20 seconds before we emerged from the other end. For about five seconds I had the strange feeling of weightlessness and an increased forward momentum. . . . I gasped to see the tunnel walls collapse and form a slit that slowly rotated clockwise.

All of our electronic and magnetic navigational instruments were malfunctioning. The compass was slowly spinning even as the airplane flew straight.

Several testimonies of those who have survived the Bermuda Triangle, say their compasses did not function properly.

Gernon said that after the fog broke apart in a weird electronic fashion, he flew into blue skies and landed in Miami about a half hour sooner than the trip would normally take.

A Squadron Disappears into Thin Air

Three months after World War II ended, on December 5, 1945, fourteen U.S. Navy air crewmen set off on a routine training flight from a naval air station in Ft. Lauderdale, FL. The morning had been uneventful—the servicemen had finished lunch and were discussing their plans for the upcoming holiday season. For the student pilots, this was to be their last practice before graduation.

Six-year Navy veteran Lt. Charles C. Taylor was leading the men. He was a well-seasoned pilot, having logged more than 2,000 hours. At about 2:00 p.m., they all boarded their five TBM

Avenger torpedo bombers and headed skyward for a three-hour exercise in which they intended to drop practice torpedoes in the Bahamas. Temperatures hovered in the mid 60s, and the weather was considered average.

At 2:15 p.m., the formation of five planes known as Flight 19 released its bombs on the shoals 22 miles north of Bimini in the Bahamas. After successfully completing the first part of the mission, the planes left the area at about 3 p.m. A fishing boat skipper later reported seeing the **squadron** flying east at about that time. Meanwhile, turbulent air and **squalls** were rolling in.

At about 3:45 p.m., another pilot in the area, Lt. Robert F. Cox, picked up a radio call from a Flight 19 plane crew asking for compass readings and indicating that they were lost. By now, the weather had turned and the airmen were facing rain, gusty winds, and low cloud cover. Immediately, Cox informed the naval air station about what he had heard. Then Cox connected via his radio with squadron leader Taylor. At 4:21 p.m., Taylor said in an anxious voice: "Both my compasses are out and I'm trying to find Ft. Lauderdale, Florida. I'm over land, but it's broken. I'm sure I'm in the Keys, but I don't know how far down."

Cox told Taylor he would fly to meet him, and a few minutes later Taylor said that his team had just passed over a small island but no other land was in sight. Cox could not understand why Taylor could not see other islands or the Florida **peninsula** if they were flying over the Keys. Then, Taylor asked for help: Could someone be sent to pick them up? He indicated that they were lost and none of the compasses seemed to be working. At that point, vessels in the area were alerted to search for the aircraft, and the Coast Guard prepared to initiate a search party. At 4:25 p.m., a call came in from another plane in Flight 19 saying that they were not sure where they were. Then another pilot radioed: "We're completely lost." At 4:28 p.m., Cox tried to make contact again but did not receive a reply. He did, however, hear the servicemen discussing their possible position and compass problems.

Cox was puzzled that Flight 19 didn't seem to be following any common emergency procedures. The pilots needed to turn on their homing devices and rise in altitude. If they were over water, they should fly west. If they were over land, they should fly east. But Flight 19 took none of these actions.

Oddly enough, Cox's radio had a malfunction and went dead, so he decided to head back to an air base and try to help from there. At 5:07 p.m., however, a radioman picked up conversation from Taylor and his men. Taylor was ordering the planes to come into a tight formation and to fly east. Other airmen urgently argued with Taylor, saying that they should turn in the other direction and head west.

When the planes had about two hours of fuel left, a new **transmission** came from Flight 19 indicating that the pilots had spotted a major island. The five planes headed west. At the naval base, their radio signals grew stronger. It appeared that the squadron was now on course and would make it home. But then at about 6:10 p.m., Taylor, still confused as to their location, changed his mind yet again. This decision obliterated their last hope. The final transmissions picked up concerned ditching the planes in the ocean unless they found land. Investigators think that one pilot became fed up, broke from the formation, and headed off on his own. Still, signals from all planes disappeared, as did each and every aircraft.

Quickly, the Navy launched rescue planes to search for the missing Flight 19. But just after 20 minutes, one of the rescue aircraft, a PBM-5 Mariner flying boat with 13 men on board, also disappeared. Merchant seamen in the area testified that they saw the plane explode, but no survivors, bodies, or **debris** were ever found.

Watch *Mystery of the Bermuda Triangle.*

Abandoned Ships

Throughout the centuries, many ships have disappeared in the region. For example, on December 30, 1812, the *Patriot* sailed from Charleston, SC, toward New York City with the daughter of former U.S. vice president Aaron Burr aboard. It was never heard from again. Then there is the story of the famous "ghost ship" the *Mary Celeste*, which may have passed through the Triangle. Ten people set sail on the ship from New York to Italy in the fall of 1872. Although it was found floating adrift off the coast of Portugal, one theory holds that the vessel might have gone off course through the Devil's Triangle before arriving in Europe with absolutely no one on board.

In 1881, a similar tale unfolded when the ship the *Ellen Austin* was sailing just south of Bermuda. The crew of that ship spotted another large vessel floating adrift. When they got near, they realized that the ship was deserted. The captain of the *Ellen Austin* sent a few his men aboard the ghost ship so they could guide it back to a port, where the captain expected to fetch a handsome payment for returning the vessel or selling it. As they sailed back to land, the crew of the *Ellen Austin* lost sight of the other ship briefly. When the other ship reappeared, it was again completely abandoned—none of the men from the *Ellen Austin* who had taken command of the vessel were to be found.

Vanishing Vessels

One of the most noted ship disappearances happened in 1918 when the USS *Cyclops* set off from Barbados in the Caribbean on March 4, scheduled to reach Baltimore, MD, on March 13. The massive carrier ship supplied fuel to the American fleet during World War I, but when it headed up the coast it was carrying more than 10,000 tons of manganese ore to be used in the production of weapons. Along the way, however, the entire ship and crew vanished without a trace. A distress call was never issued; debris was never found. A submarine or ship comman-

The USS Cyclops *in the Hudson River.*

deered by the wartime enemy, Germany, may have sunk the vessel or high winds could have capsized it. Another theory suggests that the captain was intensely disliked by his crew, and the mutinous sailors destroyed the vessel. Still, no remnant of ship or crewmember was ever found. In 1941, two ships of almost identical design to the USS *Cyclops* also vanished in the Triangle— the *Proteus* and the *Nereus*. Both vessels had been carrying bauxite, a mineral that is vital to making aircraft. The U.S. Navy speculated that German subs sunk both ships, but their wreckage has never been discovered. Similarly, a cargo ship dubbed *Sandra* went missing in 1950, as did the ship the *Southern Districts* in 1951. Bad weather or rough seas often cause shipwrecks, but neither ship sent a distress call or S.O.S. and wreckage was never discovered.

As recently as 2015 ships in the region have experienced unexplained disaster. On October 1, 2015, the SS *El Faro* was swallowed by the sea. En route from Jacksonville, FL, to Puerto Rico, the cargo ship carried 290 vehicles and 390 shipping containers, along with a crew of 33 men and women. On the first day of October, tropical storm Joaquin pummeled the ship, and the

During an underwater search mission, these images were taken of the wreckage of the SS El Faro. It was found on the seafloor, 15,000 feet deep near the Bahamas.

captain sent out a distress call that it was taking on water but the flooding was under control. Then the radio signal went silent. Rescue crews were dispatched, and a few weeks later a U.S. Navy ship discovered the *El Faro* standing upright on the ocean floor. Yet, not one crewmember was found. They were gone without a trace, and no bodies have ever turned up.

Scientific Take: Weird Natural Phenomena May Be to Blame

In the fall of 2016, the Science Channel's What on Earth? program reported that strange clouds form over the Bermuda Triangle that can create 170 mph "air bombs" or sudden hurricane-force bursts capable of sinking ships and downing planes. The researchers on this show believe that these clouds may explain the region's mysteries. Another theory is that large bubbles of methane gas may rise to the ocean's surface that either cause ships to sink quickly, or the gas may rise in the air to disable passing aircraft. A simpler explanation may be that the area is prone to sudden bursts of wild weather. Strong winds, electrical storms, and hurricanes can come up quickly. The fast swirling winds of tornadoes can form waterspouts that send water skyward. These may have the power to bring down planes or sink ships.

Alien Activity?

When the inexplicable happens, UFO believers tend to suspect that aliens are involved. On March 12, 2009, passengers aboard a flight through the Devil's Triangle spotted peculiar lights over the sea. Naval cameras also spotted the unusual lights over what looked like a vortex. The lights remained static for about an hour before fading away. When the aircraft carrier USS *John F. Kennedy* was traveling through the Triangle in 1971, members of the crew witnessed a glowing circle hovering above the ship. It hovered silently for about 20 minutes and then disappeared in a flash. Reportedly, all compasses on board stopped working while the unidentified flying object was visible.

AREA 51

The aerial view of Area 51,
a secret military facility around
the dry lake bed Groom Lake.

About 83 miles from Las Vegas in Nevada's Mojave Desert, a very secretive domestic military facility has operated for decades around a dry lake bed called Groom Lake. It is marked by WARNING signs prohibiting picture-taking or going beyond its guard gates with their flashing red lights. Since its construction in 1955, the government has repeatedly denied the installation's existence.

In the summer of 2013, the Central Intelligence Agency (CIA) released a classified report on the history of the U-2 spy plane, revealing that a military base exists there and suggesting that the base is dedicated to testing spy planes. The official name of Area 51 is the Nevada Test and Training Range and it is part of Edwards Air Force Base (formerly Nellis Air Force Base). Originally nicknamed "Paradise Ranch" to make it more attractive to workers, Area 51 got its name because the parcel of land that this secretive military base sits on is designated as number 51. Just to the north is a nuclear testing zone called Area 13, which is named in the same way.

Signs near Area 51.

Words to Understand

Drone: An unmanned aerial vehicle (UAV).

Extraterrestrial: A hypothetical or fictional being from outer space, especially an intelligent one. An alien.

Hybrid: An entity made by combining two different elements or beings.

Area 51 in Pop Culture

Fictional accounts in TV, movies, and books have helped maintain the rumors of aliens and Area 51. The television show *The X-Files* had a recurring plot about alien secret technology and experiments being conducted at Area 51. In the movie *Independence Day*, the military uses alien technology captured at Roswell to launch an attack from Area 51 on the invaders. The Men in Black, made famous by Tommy Lee Jones and Will Smith in the movie by the same name, are government agents who track, threaten, and harass UFO witnesses and work in partnership with secret bases such as Area 51.

Watch the National Geographic documentary on Area 51.

A Base for UFO and Alien Research?

Over the decades since it opened, Area 51 has gained mythic status due to rumors that the military was developing advanced aircraft and weaponry there based on alien technology. People who worked there (or at least said they worked there) have added support to the claims—saying that the military had gathered technology from alien aircraft that had crashed.

Fringe researchers claim to have evidence of underground alien baby labs, and underground rooms brimming with alien technology and **extraterrestrial** specimens, but no peer-reviewed evidence has ever come to light. More outrageous theories center around the idea that the government may be trying to create alien-human **hybrids**. The fact that the secretive installation does develop and test experimental aircraft may have fueled the idea that Area 51 is connected to UFOs and alien life, although definitive proof of alien life has yet to be found.

Scientific Take: Testing Secret Aircraft

The 2013 report released by the CIA about the U-2 spy plane explains how reports of UFOs grew in connection to Area 51: "High-altitude testing of the U-2 soon led to an unexpected

A U-2 spy plane lands on the dry lake after flight.

side-effect—a tremendous increase in reports of unidentified flying objects. U-2 and later Ox-cart [a successor to the U-2] flights accounted for more than one-half of all UFO reports during the late 1950s and most of the 1960s." When locals saw the strange aircraft speeding overhead, the plane looked so alien it was thought to be from another world.

Stories of Extraterrestrials

Over the decades eyewitnesses have provided many accounts of alien aircraft shining strange lights and flying in unusual patterns in the sky. With new helicopters, airplanes, and unmanned

A Bizarre Russian Propaganda Effort?

American journalist Annie Jacobsen, in the book *Area 51: An Uncensored History of America's Top Secret Military Base*, presents one of the wilder theories behind the Roswell crash. She wrote that the crashed flying saucer was not piloted by extraterrestrials, but rather by young teenage Russian children whose bodies had been surgically re-engineered to make them look like aliens. Jacobsen stated that Josef Stalin ordered that these human guinea pigs be flown to America with the hopes that they would cause panic in the United States.

Although drones are an interesting development in technology, they have confused some people who mistake them for UFOs.

drones flying near the military facility, it is no wonder that those who have spotted aircraft may have interpreted them as alien technology. Pat Travis, who operates the Little A'Le'Inn in Rachel, NV, near Area 51, said that she was awakened one night by a bright light that came through the center of the back door, shot from a UFO. Online, many photos and videos are posted of inexplicable lights flying in the night skies over the desert. In December of 2014, a Utah man reported that while hiking near Area 51 he recorded strange lights appearing and disappearing.

In October of that same year, the *Daily Mail* reported that a scientist, Boyd Bushman, who had worked for Lockheed Martin and at Area 51, said that he personally could confirm that extraterrestrials were in Area 51. (He also believed that the aliens, who were about five feet tall and had fingers and toes like us, came from a planet called Quintumnia. Although located 68 light-years away, the aliens could make the journey to Earth in 45 minutes.) In the late 1980s, American businessman and scientist Robert Lazar told a television station that he had worked on crashed flying saucers at Area 51. The entire story was a fabrication, but it spurred the belief that the base was connected to UFOs.

The Roswell Incident

Like Area 51, Roswell, NM, is another location deeply connected to alien rumors. During the first week of July 1947, an unidentified flying object crashed northwest of the town on a ranch owned by Mac Brazel. While officials from the local Air Force base maintained that it was a weather balloon, eyewitnesses said the material strewn over the ranch did not look like one. After military personnel fanned out over the ranch and quickly whisked away all evidence, rumors began that alien aircraft had crashed there.

Years later, an Air Force report stated that the crashed aircraft was part of Project Mogul, a plan to develop high-altitude balloons carrying low-frequency sound sensors. Many people, however, suspected that the government and military had been covering up what really happened—an alien crash. Roswell is a long distance from Area 51, just under 900 miles, but the two locations have been linked by alien lore. UFO investigators claim that alien spacecraft wreckage from Roswell was shipped to Area 51 for examination, and according to some believers, actual alien bodies were recovered from the crash site and taken to Area 51, where autopsies were performed.

The front page of the Roswell Daily Record (left) on July 8, 1947 After the Roswell Incident, museums popped up to commemorate the event. This exhibit (above) shows the supposed autopsies that were performed on alien bodies.

Series Glossary

Affliction: Something that causes pain or suffering.

Afterlife: Life after death.

Anthropologist: A professional who studies the origin, development, and behavioral aspects of human beings and their societies, especially primitive societies.

Apparition: A ghost or ghostlike image of a person.

Archaeologist: A person who studies human history and prehistory through the excavation of sites and the analysis of artifacts and other physical remains found.

Automaton: A person who acts in a mechanical, machinelike way as if in trance.

Bipolar disorder: A mental condition marked by alternating periods of elation and depression.

Catatonic: To be in a daze or stupor.

Celestial: Relating to the sky or heavens.

Charlatan: A fraud.

Chronic: Continuing for a long time; used to describe an illness or medical condition generally lasting longer than three months.

Clairvoyant: A person who claims to have a supernatural ability to perceive events in the future or beyond normal sensory contact.

Cognition: The mental action or process of acquiring knowledge and understanding through thought, experience, and the senses.

Déjà vu: A sensation of experiencing something that has happened before when experienced for the first time.

Delirium: A disturbed state of mind characterized by confusion, disordered speech, and hallucinations.

Dementia: A chronic mental condition caused by brain disease or injury and characterized by memory disorders, personality changes, and impaired reasoning.

Dissociative: Related to a breakdown of mental function that normally operates smoothly, such as memory and consciousness. Dissociative identity disorder is a mental Trauma: A deeply distressing or disturbing experience.

Divine: Relating to God or a god.

Ecstatic: A person subject to mystical experiences.

Elation: Great happiness.

Electroencephalogram (EEG): A test that measures and records the electrical activity of the brain.

Endorphins: Hormones secreted within the brain and nervous system that trigger a positive feeling in the body.

ESP (extrasensory perception): An ability to communicate or understand outside of normal sensory capability, such as in telepathy and clairvoyance.

Euphoria: An intense state of happiness; elation.

Hallucinate: To experience a perception of something that seems real but is not actually present.

Immortal: Living forever.

Inhibition: A feeling that makes one self-conscious and unable to act in a relaxed and natural way.

Involuntary: Not subject to a person's control.

Karma: A Buddhist belief that whatever one does comes back—a person's actions can determine his or her reincarnation.

Levitate: To rise in the air by supernatural or magical power.

Malevolent: Evil.

Malignant: Likely to grow and spread in a fast and uncontrolled way that can cause death.

Mayhem: Chaos.

Mesmerize: To hold someone's attention so that he or she notices nothing else.

Mindfulness: A meditation practice for bringing one's attention to the internal and external experiences occurring in the present moment.

Monolith: A giant, single upright block of stone, especially as a monument.

Motivational: Designed to promote a willingness to do or achieve something.

Motor functions: Muscle and nerve acts that produce motion. Fine motor functions include writing and tying shoes; gross motor functions are large movements such as walking and kicking.

Mystics: People who have supernatural knowledge or experiences; they have a supposed insight into spirituality and mysteries transcending ordinary human knowledge.

Necromancy: An ability to summon and control things that are dead.

Neurological: Related to the nervous system or neurology (a branch of medicine concerning diseases and disorders of the nervous system).

Neuroplasticity: The ability of the brain to form and reorganize synaptic connections, especially in response to learning or experience, or following injury.

Neuroscientist: One who studies the nervous system

Neurotransmitters: Chemicals released by nerve fibers that transmit signals across a synapse (the gap between nerve cells).

Occult: Of or relating to secret knowledge of supernatural things.

Olfactory: Relating to the sense of smell.

Out-of-body experience: A sensation of being outside one's body, floating above and observing events, often when unconscious or clinically dead.

Papyrus: A material prepared in ancient Egypt from the pithy stem of a water plant, used to make sheets for writing or painting on, rope, sandals, and boats.

Paralysis: An inability to move or act.

Paranoid: Related to a mental condition involving intense anxious or fearful feelings and thoughts often related to persecution, threat, or conspiracy.

Paranormal: Beyond the realm of the normal; outside of commonplace scientific understanding.

Paraphysical: Not part of the physical word; often used in relation to supernatural occurrences.

Parapsychologist: A person who studies paranormal and psychic phenomena.

Parapsychology: Study of paranormal and psychic phenomena considered inexplicable in the world of traditional psychology.

Phobia: Extreme irrational fear.

Physiologist: A person who studies the workings of living systems.

Precognition: Foreknowledge of an event through some sort of ESP.

Premonition: A strong feeling that something is about to happen, especially something unpleasant.

Pseudoscience: Beliefs or practices that may appear scientific, but have not been proven by any scientific method.

Psychiatric: Related to mental illness or its treatment.

Psychic: Of or relating to the mind; often used to describe mental powers that science cannot explain.

Psychokinesis: The ability to move or manipulate objects using the mind alone.

Psychological: Related to the mental and emotional state of a person.

PTSD: Post-traumatic stress disorder is a mental health condition triggered by a terrifying event.

Repository: A place, receptacle, or structure where things are stored.

Resilient: Able to withstand or recover quickly from difficult conditions.

Resonate: To affect or appeal to someone in a personal or emotional way.

Schizophrenia: A severe mental disorder characterized by an abnormal grasp of reality; symptoms can include hallucinations and delusions.

Skeptic: A person who questions or doubts particular things.

Spectral: Ghostly.

Spiritualism: A religious movement that believes the spirits of the dead can communicate with the living.

Stimulus: Something that causes a reaction.

Subconscious: The part of the mind that we are not aware of but that influences our thoughts, feelings, and behaviors.

Sumerians: An ancient civilization/people (5400–1750 BCE) in the region known as Mesopotamia (modern day Iraq and Kuwait).

Synapse: A junction between two nerve cells.

Synthesize: To combine a number of things into a coherent whole.

Telekinesis: Another term for psychokinesis. The ability to move or manipulate objects using the mind alone.

Telepathy: Communication between people using the mind alone and none of the five senses.

Uncanny: Strange or mysterious.

Further Resources

Websites

Easter Island Foundation: *http://islandheritage.org/wordpress/*
This organization has a mission to build a library on Easter Island and promote awareness of the island's fragile heritage.

English Heritage: Stonehenge: *http://www.english-heritage.org.uk/visit/places/stonehenge/*
English Heritage cares for over 400 historic buildings, monuments, and sites. This site is dedicated to Stonehenge and current events and policies at the site.

Great Pyramid of Giza Research Association: *http://www.gizapyramid.com/*
The world's largest research association and leading web site for information on the Great Pyramid of Giza.

Mutual UFO Network (MUFON) : *http://www.mufon.com/alien-technology/how-area-51-works*
This site tracks recent UFO sightings, daily UFO sightings, alien news, and alien encounters, including information related to Area 51.

National Oceanic and Atmospheric Association , U.S. Department of Commerce
http://oceanservice.noaa.gov/facts/bermudatri.html
This is a science-based federal agency that provides further information on the Bermuda Triangle.

Movies

Here are a few movies that feature mysterious places:

Area 51 **(2015)**
Three young conspiracy theorists attempt to uncover the mysteries of Area 51.

Minions **(2015)**
The spin-off/prequel to *Despicable Me* reveals that the minions build the Great Pyramid.

Tess **(1979)**
Roman Polanski's adaptation of the classic Thomas Hardy novel Tess of the d'Urbervilles features a dramatic scene at Stonehenge.

Further Reading

Allman, Toney. *The Mysterious & Unknown: Stonehenge.* San Diego: Reference Point Press, 2008.

Belanger, Jeff. *The Mysteries of the Bermuda Triangle.* New York: Grosset & Dunlap, 2010.

Chrisp, Peter. *DK Experience: Pyramid.* New York: DK Children, 2006.

Higgins, Nadia. *Area 51 (Unexplained Mysteries).* Hopkins, MN: Bellweather Media, 2014.

Hill, Rosemary. *Stonehenge.* Cambridge, MA: Harvard University, 2008.

Hunt, Terry and Carl Lipo. *The Statues That Walked: Unraveling the Mystery of Easter Island.* Berkeley, CA: Counterpoint, 2012.

Jacobsen, Annie. *Area 51: An Uncensored History of America's Top Secret Military Base.* New York: Little Brown and Company, 2011.

Kallen, Stuart. *Pyramids.* San Diego: Lucent Books, 2002.

Reis, Ronald. *The Lost World of Easter Island.* New York: Chelsea House, 2012.

Walker, Kathryn. *Unsolved! Mysteries of the Bermuda Triangle.* London: Crabtree Publishing Company, 2009.

Sacks, Oliver. The Man Who Mistook His Wife for a Hat. New York: Touchstone Edition/Simon & Schuster, 1998.

About the Author

Don Rauf has written more than 30 nonfiction books, including *Killer Lipstick and Other Spy Gadgets, Simple Rules for Card Games, Psychology of Serial Killers: Historical Serial Killers, The French and Indian War, The Rise and Fall of the Ottoman Empire,* and *George Washington's Farewell Address.* He has contributed to the books *Weird Canada* and *American Inventions.* He lives in Seattle with his wife, Monique, and son, Leo.

Index